More Ziegfeld Girls Coloring Book

By Camilla Starfire

I0482557

This book contains 18 (plus one bonus) erotic colorable images of Ziegfeld Girls in gray scale. These images are best colored with colored pencil.

There are two ways to color gray scale images. The easiest way is to simply color over the images lightly allowing some of the underlying shading to show through. For these Ziegfeld Girls images, lightly color over the faces and other areas of skin with a flesh colored pencil. Then color over the clothes and background with the colors of your choice.

The second way of coloring gray scale images is a little more challenging. You can blend the lighter and darker areas of flesh with lighter and darker flesh colored pencils using the underlying light and dark of the print as a guide. For the clothes and background, experiment with blending lighter and darker colors in the areas that you see lighter and darker shading.

Either method or a combination of the two can give you a beautiful result.

Please note: Where I have found information on individual women, it will be on the back of their photo. I thought you might want to separate the pages from the book, and that way the information will be with that photo.

Florenz Edward Ziegfeld, Jr., popularly known as Flo Ziegfeld, was an American Broadway impresario, notable for his series of theatrical revues, the Ziegfeld Follies, inspired by the Folies Bergère of Paris. He also produced the musical Show Boat The Follies were lavish revues something between later Broadway shows and a more elaborate high class Vaudeville variety shows Many of the top entertainers of the era (including W. C, Fields, Eddie Cantor, Josephine Baker, Fanny Brice, Anne Pennington, Bert Williams, Eva Tanguay, Bob Hope, Will Rogers, Ruth Etting, Ray Bolger, Helen Morgan, Louise Brooks, Marilyn Miller, Ed Wynn, Gilda Gray, Nora Bayes, Sophie Tucker, and others) appeared in the shows. You might be surprised to find included in this list of Ziegfeld girls; Barbara Stanwick, Lana Turner, Talullah Bankhead and Gloria Swanson. The first Follies was produced in 1907 at the roof theatre Jardin de Paris. The Ziegfeld girls "paraded up and down flights of stairs as anything from birds to battleships." The Tableau Vivants were designed by Ben Ali Haggin from 1917 to 1925. Joseph Urban was the scenic designer for the Follies shows starting in 1915. After Ziegfeld's death his widow, Billie Burke authorized use of his name for Ziegfeld Follies in 1934 and 1936 to Jake Shubert, who then produced the Follies. The name was later used by other promoters in New York City, Philadelphia and again on Broadway, with less connection to the original Follies. These latter efforts failed miserably. When later it toured, the 1934 edition was recorded in its entirety, from the Overture to Play-out music, on a series of 78 rpm discs, which were edited by the record producer David Cunnard to form an album of the highlights of the production and which was released as a Compact Disc in 1997.

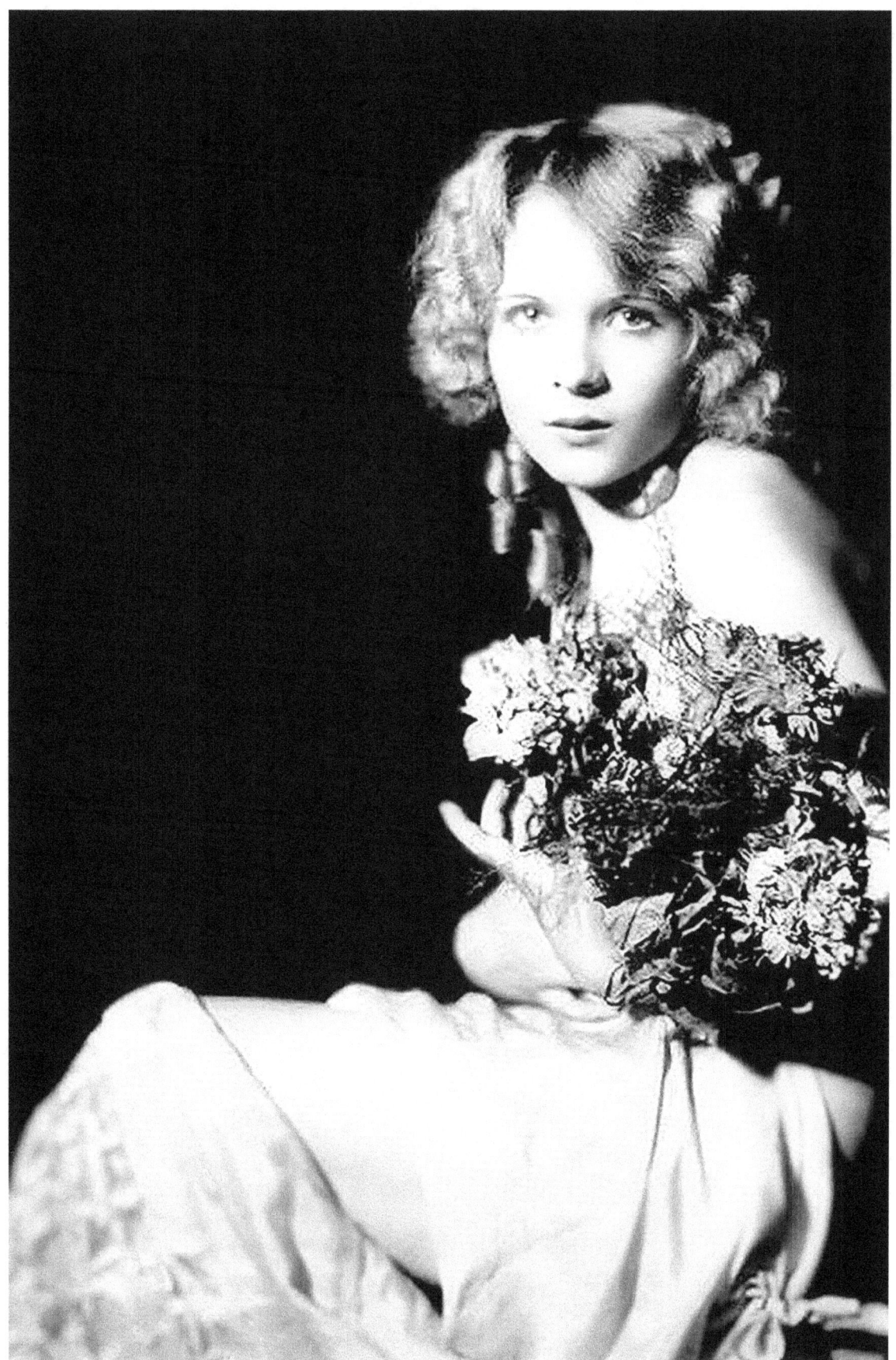

Ziegfeld girl with flowers.

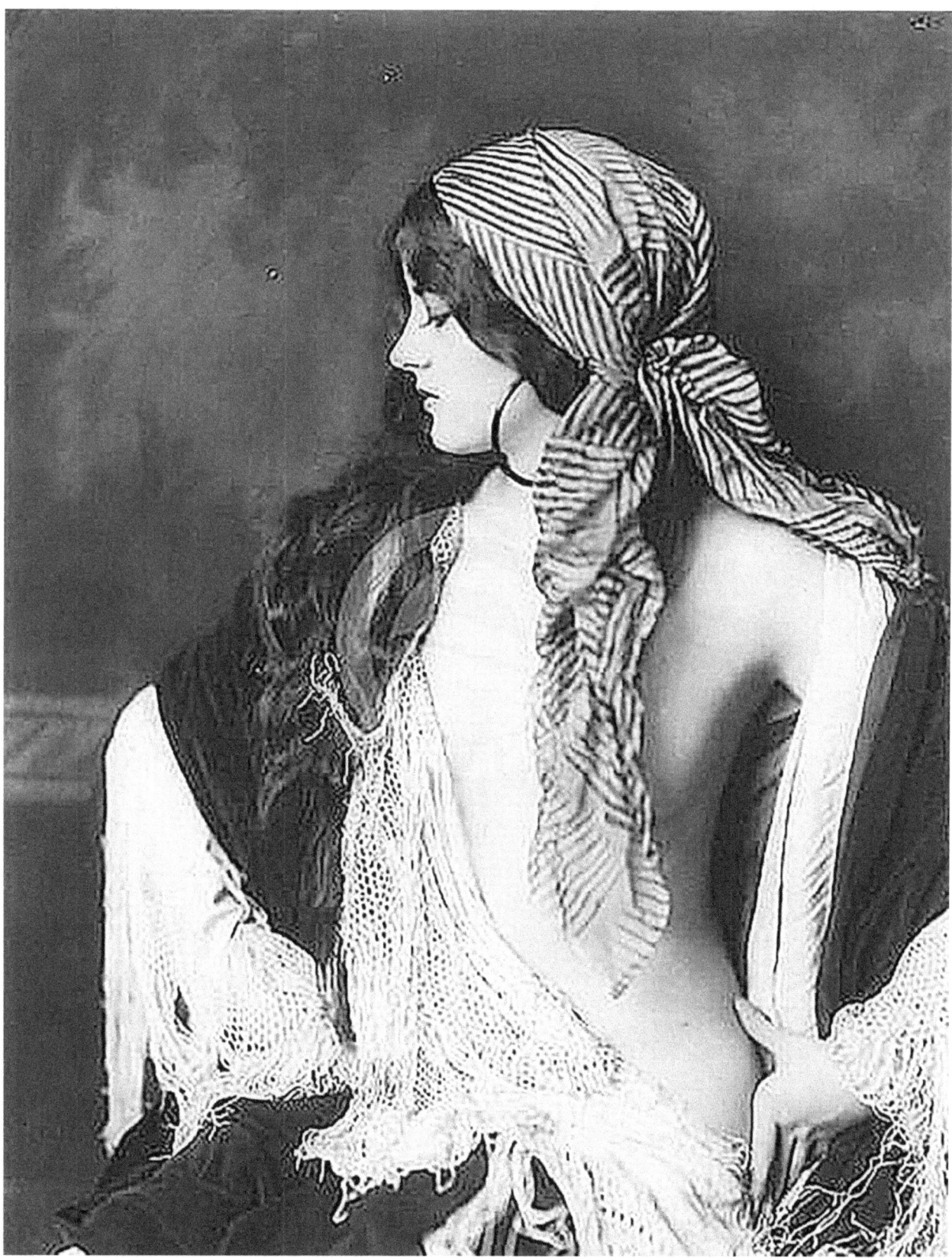

Ziegfeld girl gypsy theme

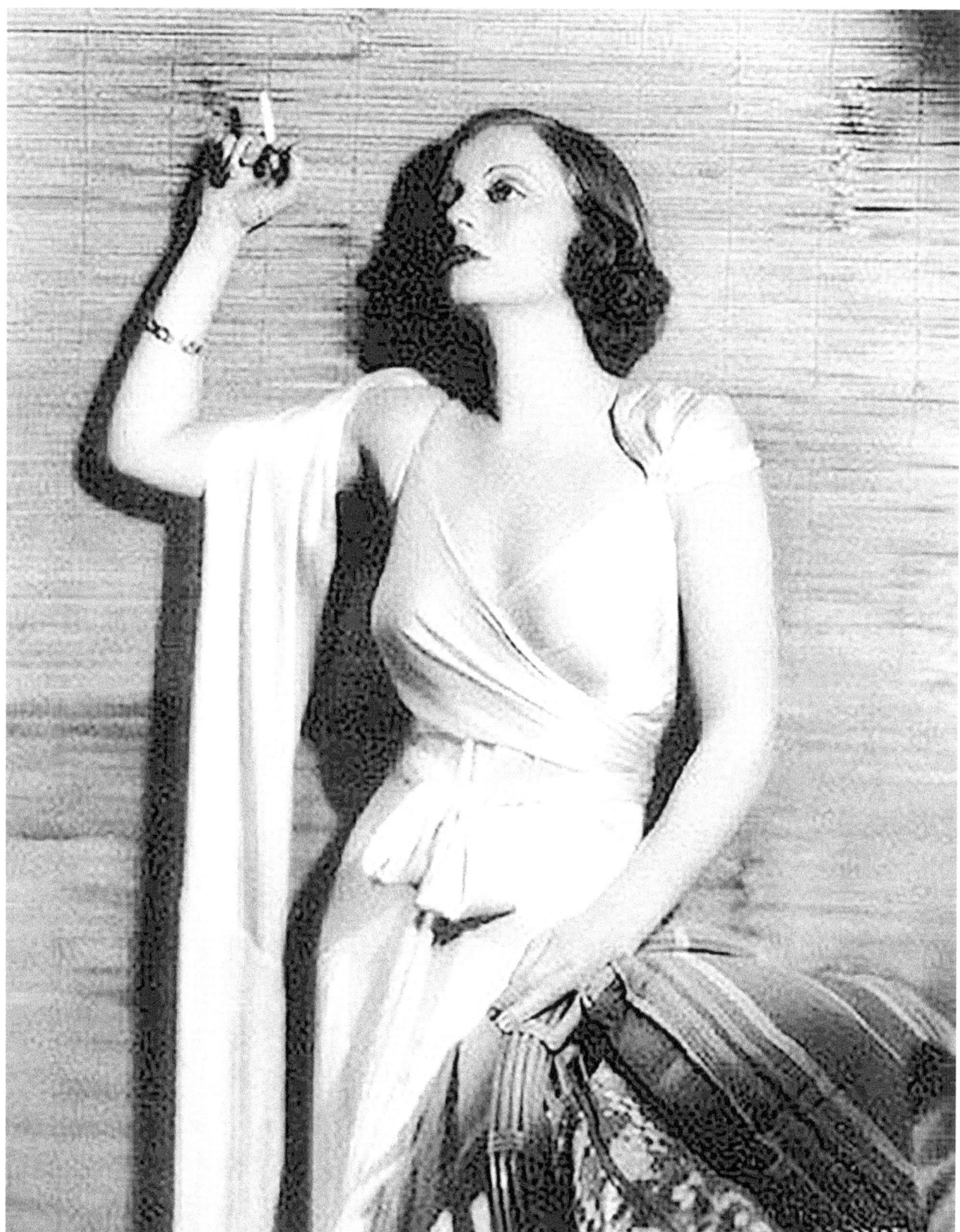

Tallulah Bankhead- Tallulah wanted to star in a revue and quickly signed on for *The Ziegfeld Follies* (bearing no resemblance to the original production). She appeared in a variety of skits and recited Dorothy Parker's poem, "The Waltz". Although she looked fabulous, her health was beginning to show the effects from years of smoking and drinking. Her dressing room was located close to the stage, so that she did not have to climb stairs, and an understudy was assigned as well. It was an expensive production with extravagant sets, but the reviews were terrible and it failed to reach Broadway.

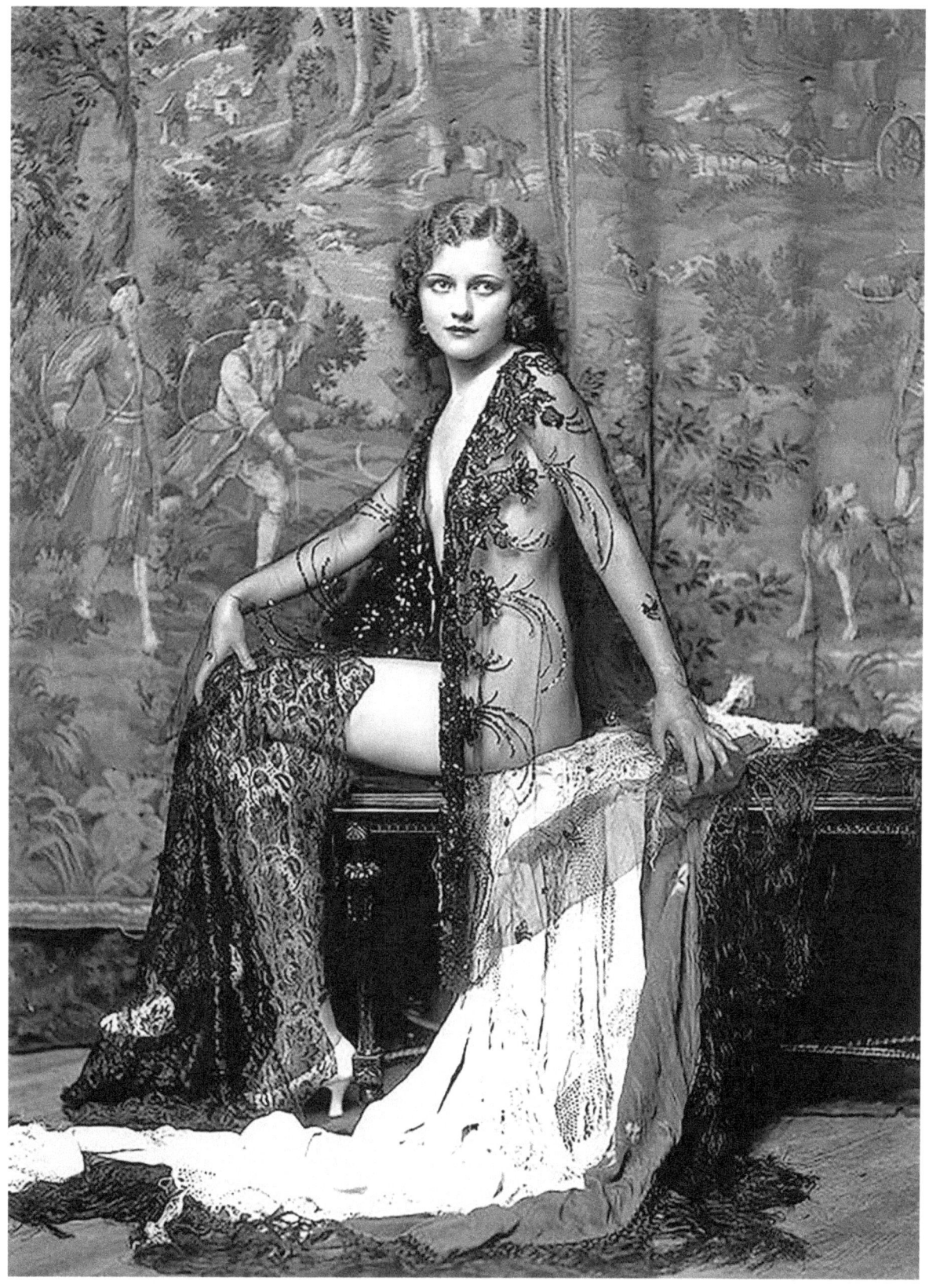

Anne Lee Patterson (aka: Anne L. Bandler) She was not really interested in being an actress, but did enjoy modeling and Beauty pageants, often times these pageants awarded a stage contract in which she was awarded in 1931 as a Follies Girl who prior was crowned 'Miss Northern Kentucky' which got her entry to Miss USA which she won in 1931, and, after 2nd runner up in the 1932 Miss Universe pageant (*Lost to Belgium's Miss Netta Duchâteau*

 She attended St James Elementary School as a child and later the LaSalette Academy in Covington. Moved to Bel Air California after her marriage and stayed there till her death. She had two sons.

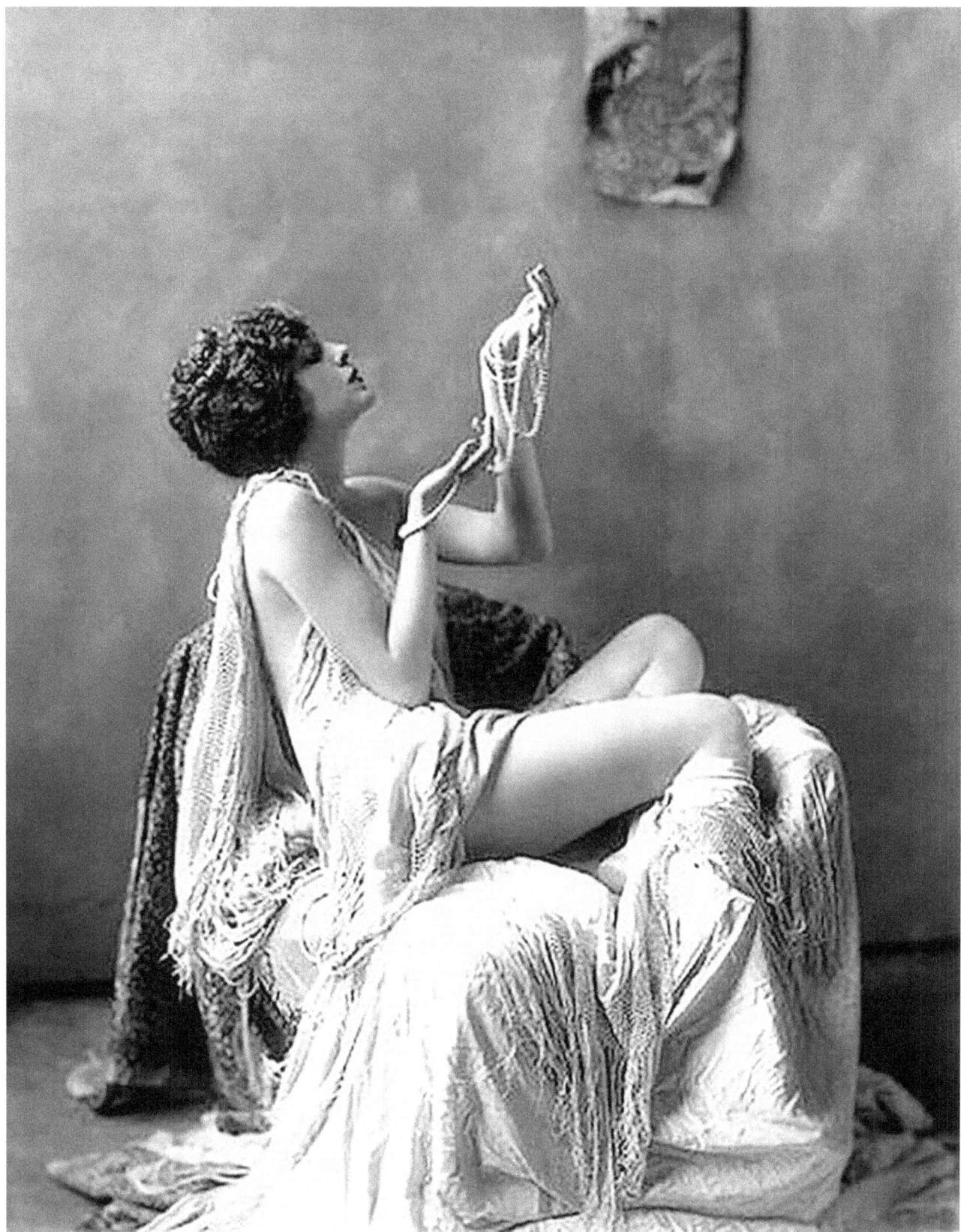

Billie Dove was born **Bertha Bohny** in 1903 to Charles and Bertha (née Kagl) Bohny, Swiss immigrants. As a teen, she worked as a model to help support her family and was hired as a teenager byFlorenz Ziegfeld to appear in his Ziegfeld Follies Revue. She legally changed her name to **Lillian Bohny** in the early 1920s and moved to Hollywood, where she began appearing in silent films. She soon became one of the most popular actresses of the 1920s, appearing in Douglas Fairbanks' smash hit Technicolor film The Black Pirate (1926), as Rodeo West in *The Painted Angel* (1929), and was dubbed The American Beauty (1927), the title of one of her films.

She married the director of her seventh film, Irvin Willat in 1923. The two divorced in 1929. Dove had a huge legion of male fans, one of her most persistent being Howard Hughes. She had a three-year romance with Hughes and was engaged to marry him, but she ended the relationship without ever giving cause. Hughes cast her as a comedian in his film *Cock of the Air* (1932). She also appeared in his movie *The Age for Love* (1931).

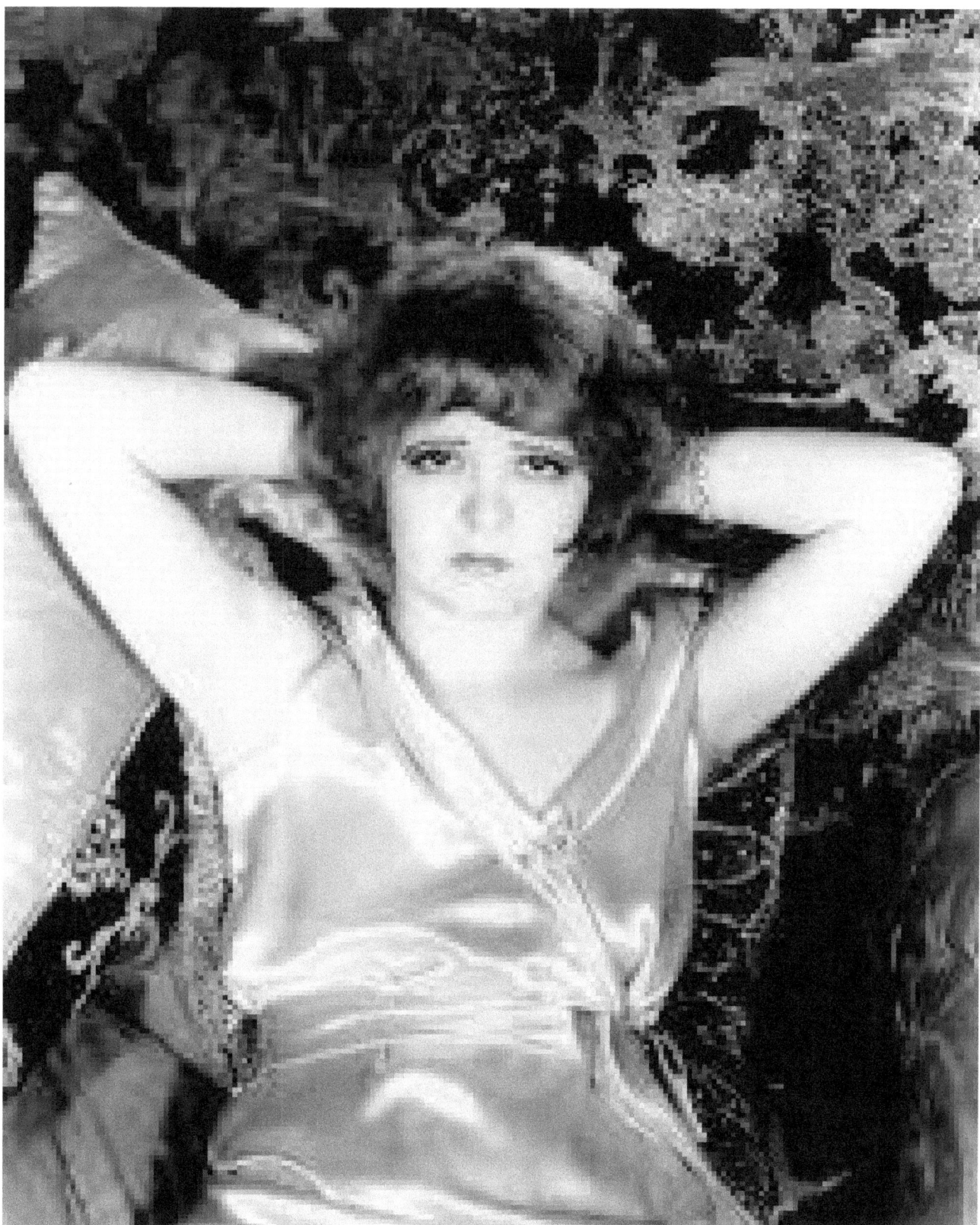

Clara Bow

Clara Gordon Bow (July 29, 1905 – September 27, 1965) was an American actress who rose to stardom in silent film during the 1920s and successfully made the transition to talkies" after 1927. Her appearance as a plucky shopgirl in the film *It* brought her global fame and the nickname "the IT girl". Bow came to personify the Roaring Twenties and is described as its leading sex symbol.

She appeared in 46 silent films and 11 talkies, including hits such as *Mantrap* (1926), *It* (1927), and *Wings* (1927). She was named first box-office draw in 1928 and 1929 and second box-office draw in 1927 and 1930. Her presence in a motion picture was said to have ensured investors, by odds of almost two-to-one, a "safe return". At the apex of her stardom, she received more than 45,000 fan letters in a single month (January 1929).

After marrying actor Res Bell in 1931, Bow retired from acting and became a rancher in Nevada. Her final film, Hoop-La was released in 1933. In September 1965, Bow died of a heart attack.at the age of 60.

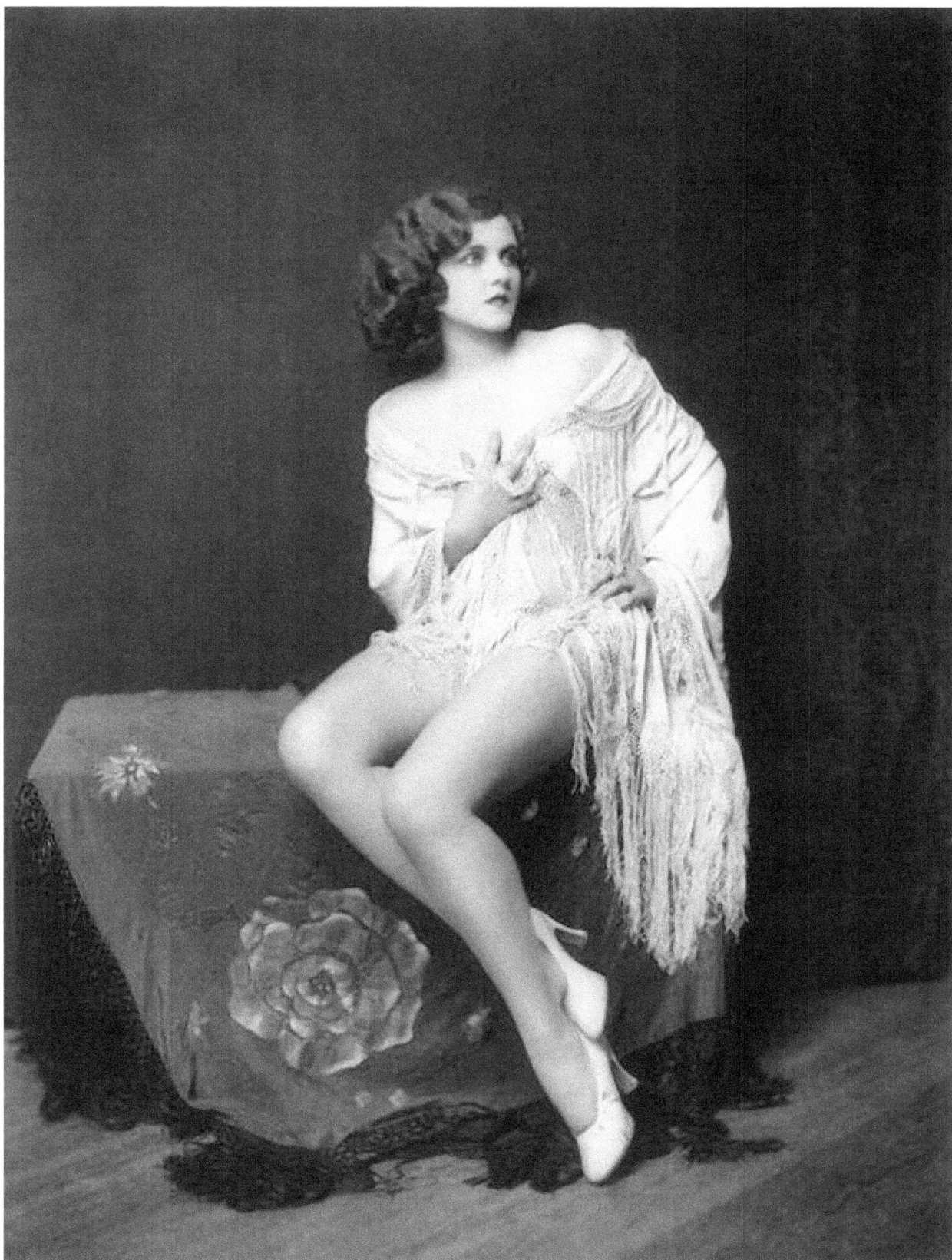

Mary Lange- Mary Lange was born on July 2, 1912 in Carnegie, Pennsylvania, USA. She was an actress, known for Poor Little Rich Boy (1932), The Great Ziegfeld (1936) and Dames (1934). She was married to Francis Kolb, a sales executive for Standard Oil. She died on April 15, 1973 in Coral Gables, Florida, USA.

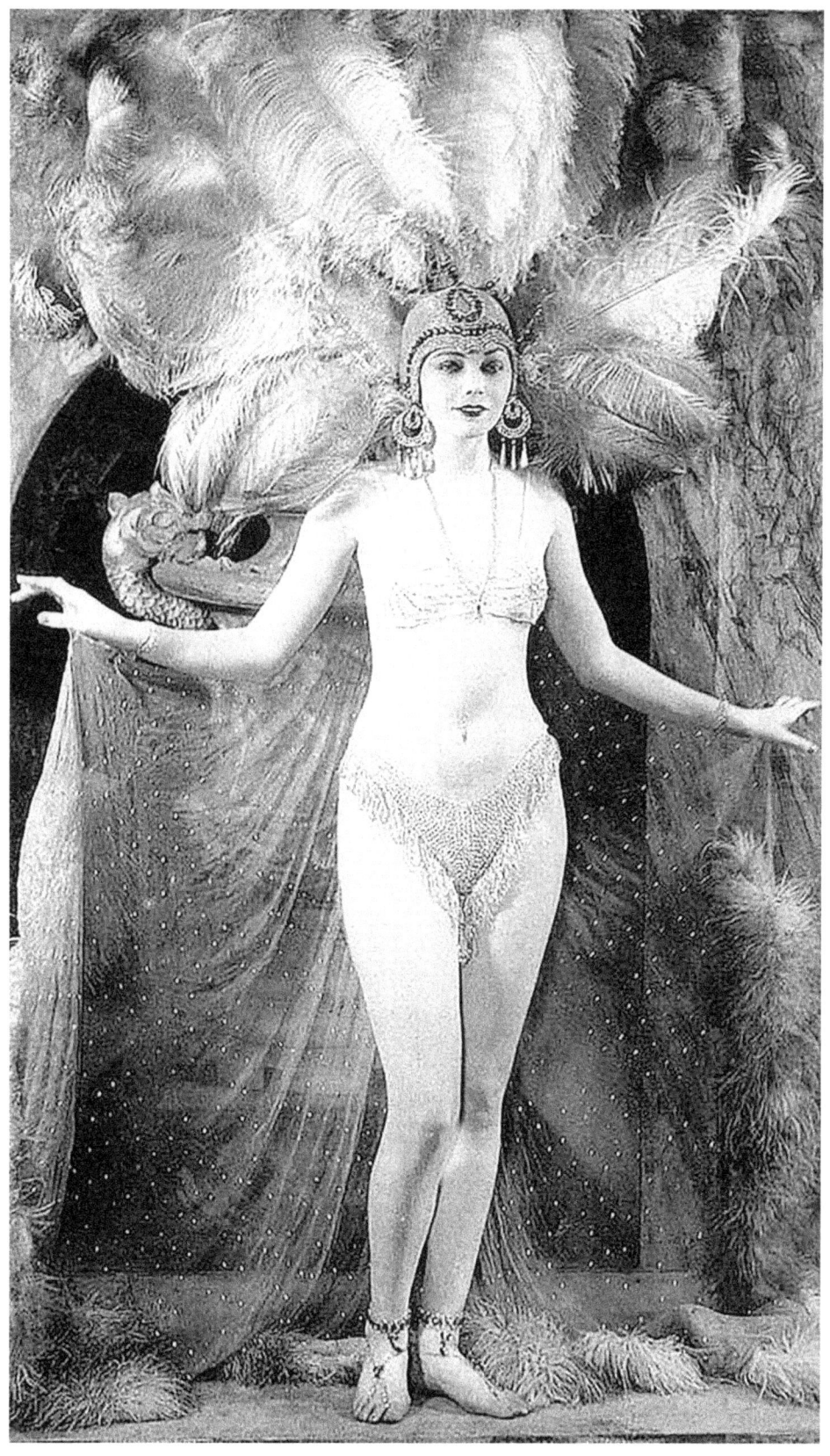

Ziegfeld girl in feathers and veils, a popular theme

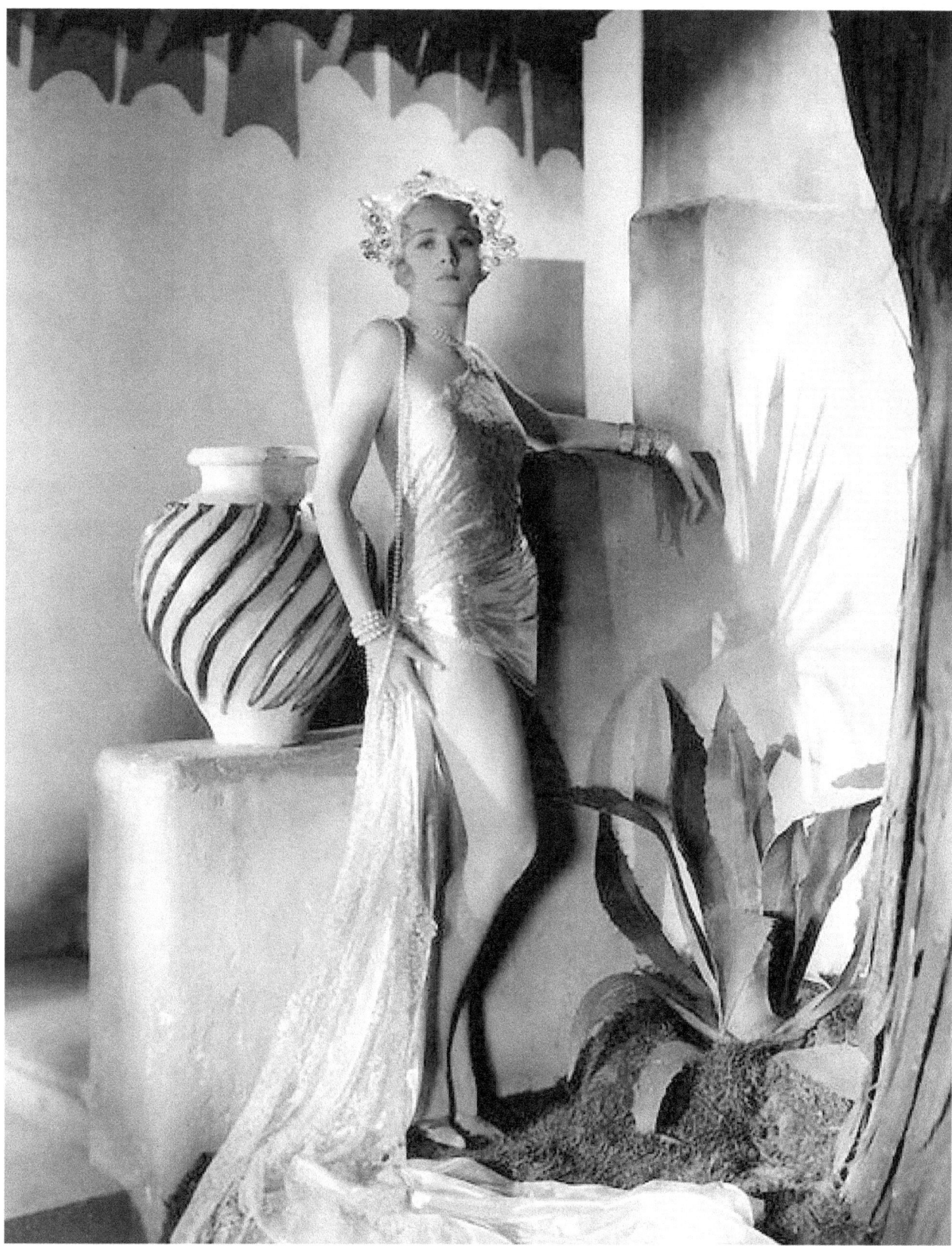

Muriel Finlay Muriel Finley was born on June 15, 1902 in Salmon, Idaho, USA. She was an actress, known for Sin Takes a Holiday (1930) and Whoopee! (1930). She died in October 1975 in Kansas City, Missouri, USA.

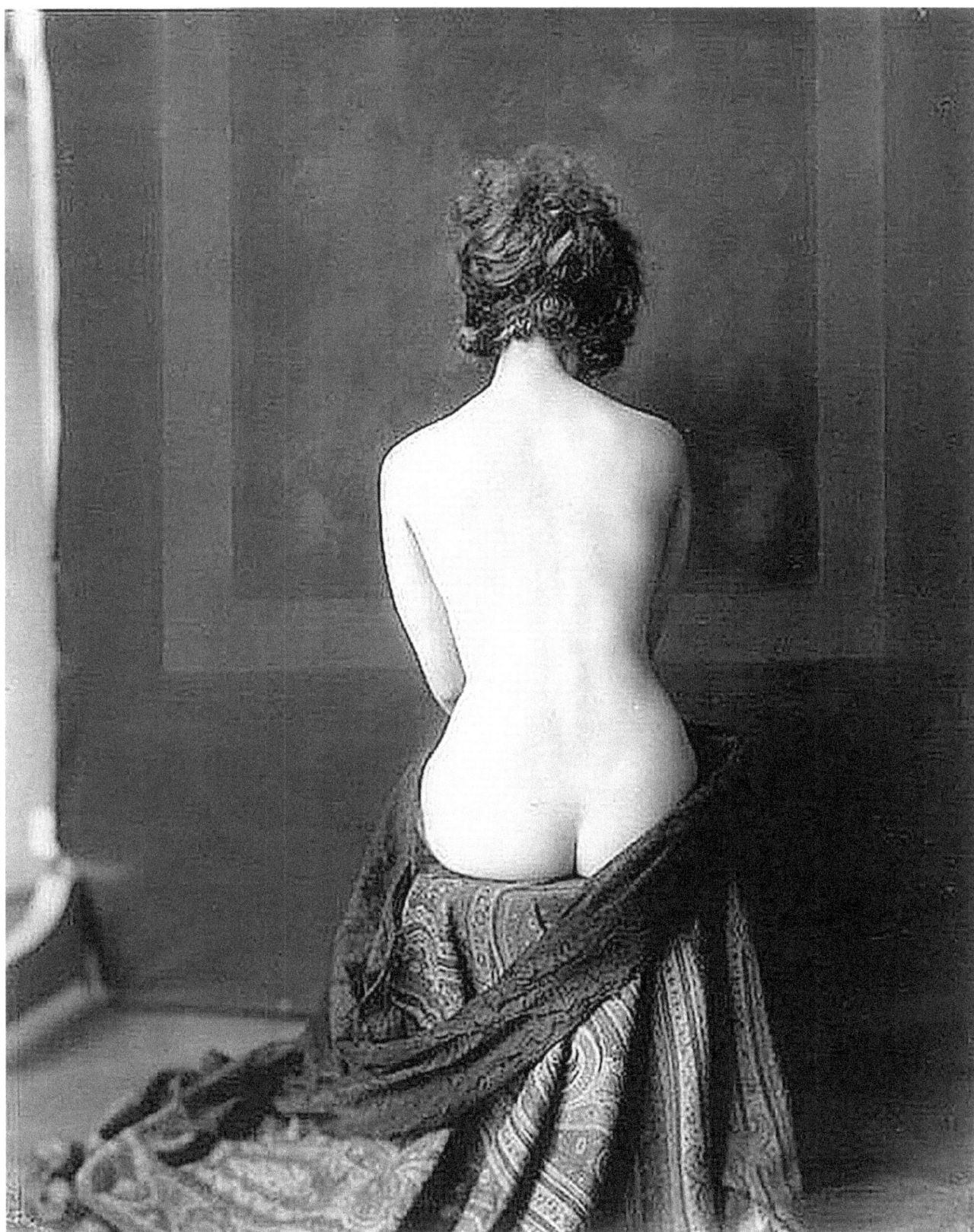

Ziegfeld girl in an elegant pose.

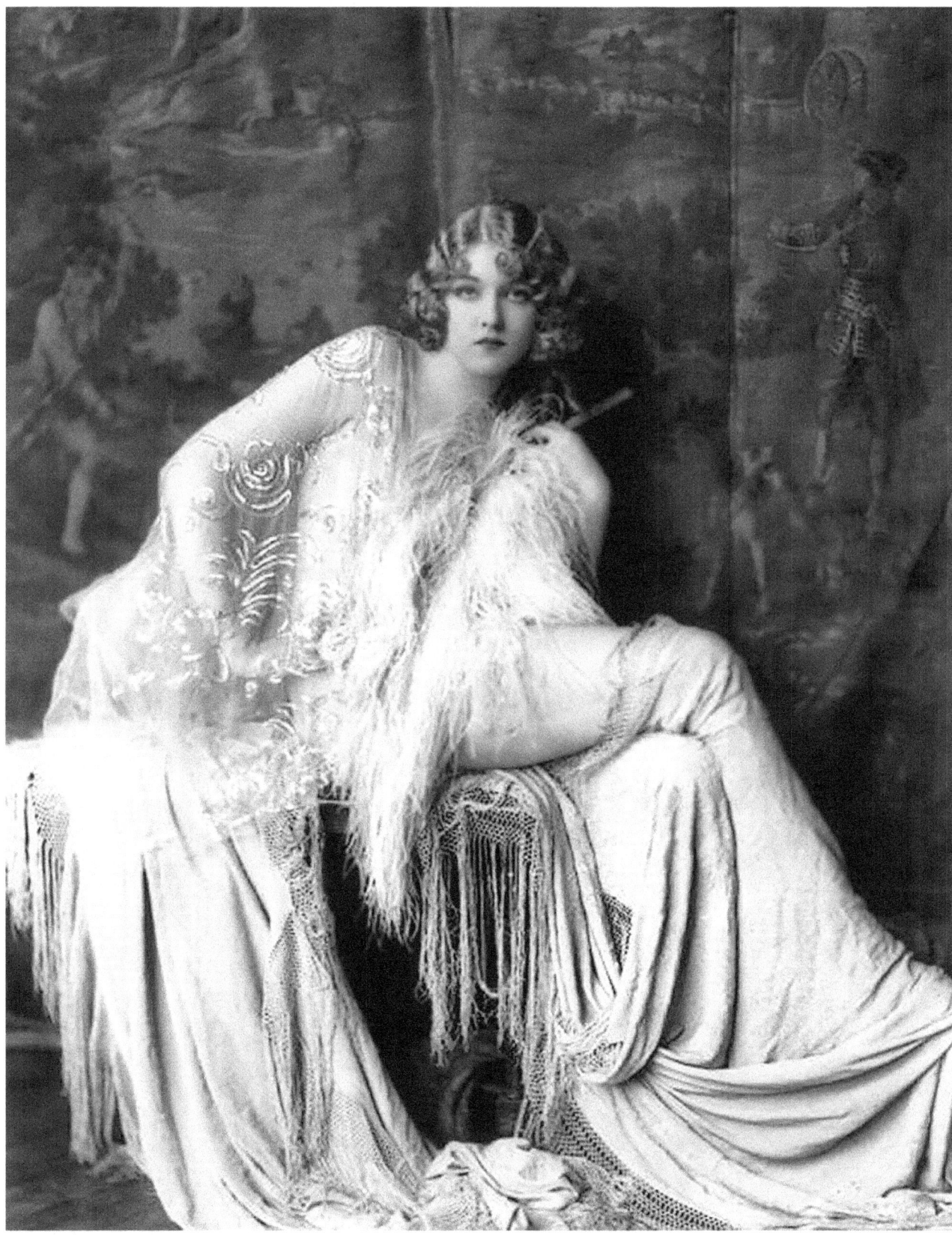

Ziegfeld girl in feathers, veils and drapes. Zeigfeld thought the draped costumes accentuated the female form. Very dramatic and elegant.

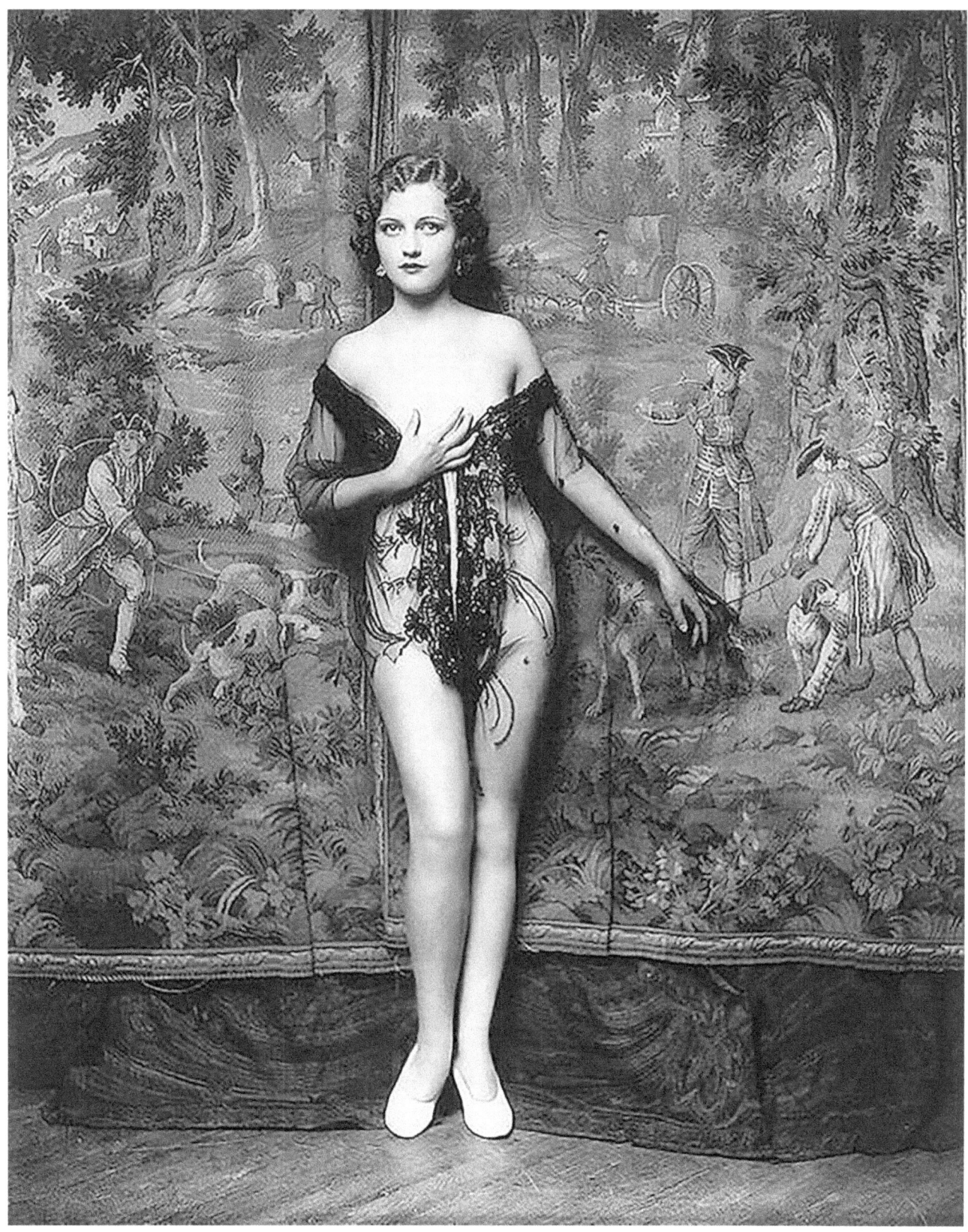

Ziegfeld girl posed in front of a detailed tapestry, a popular theme.

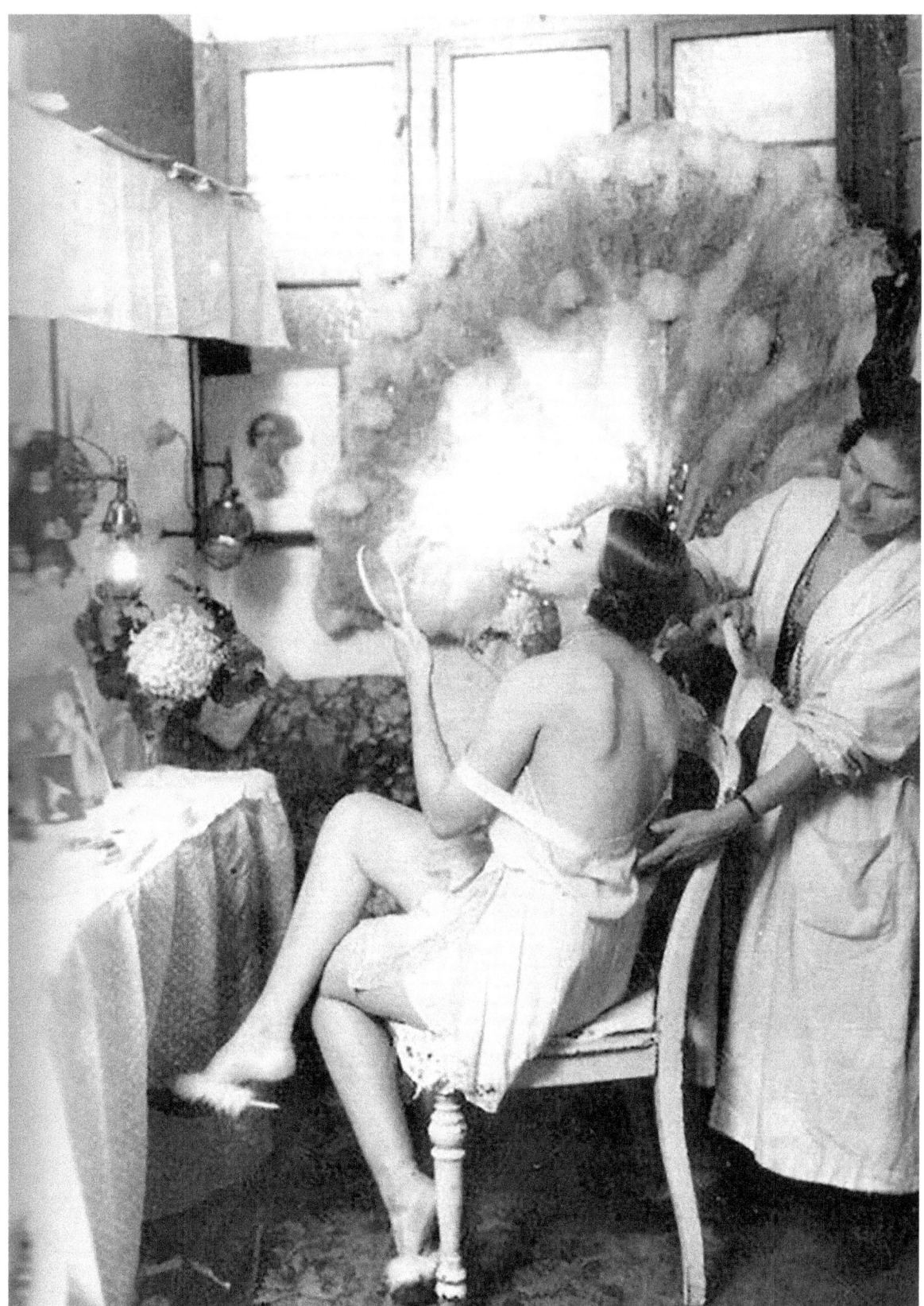

Ziegfeld girl getting ready for the stage.

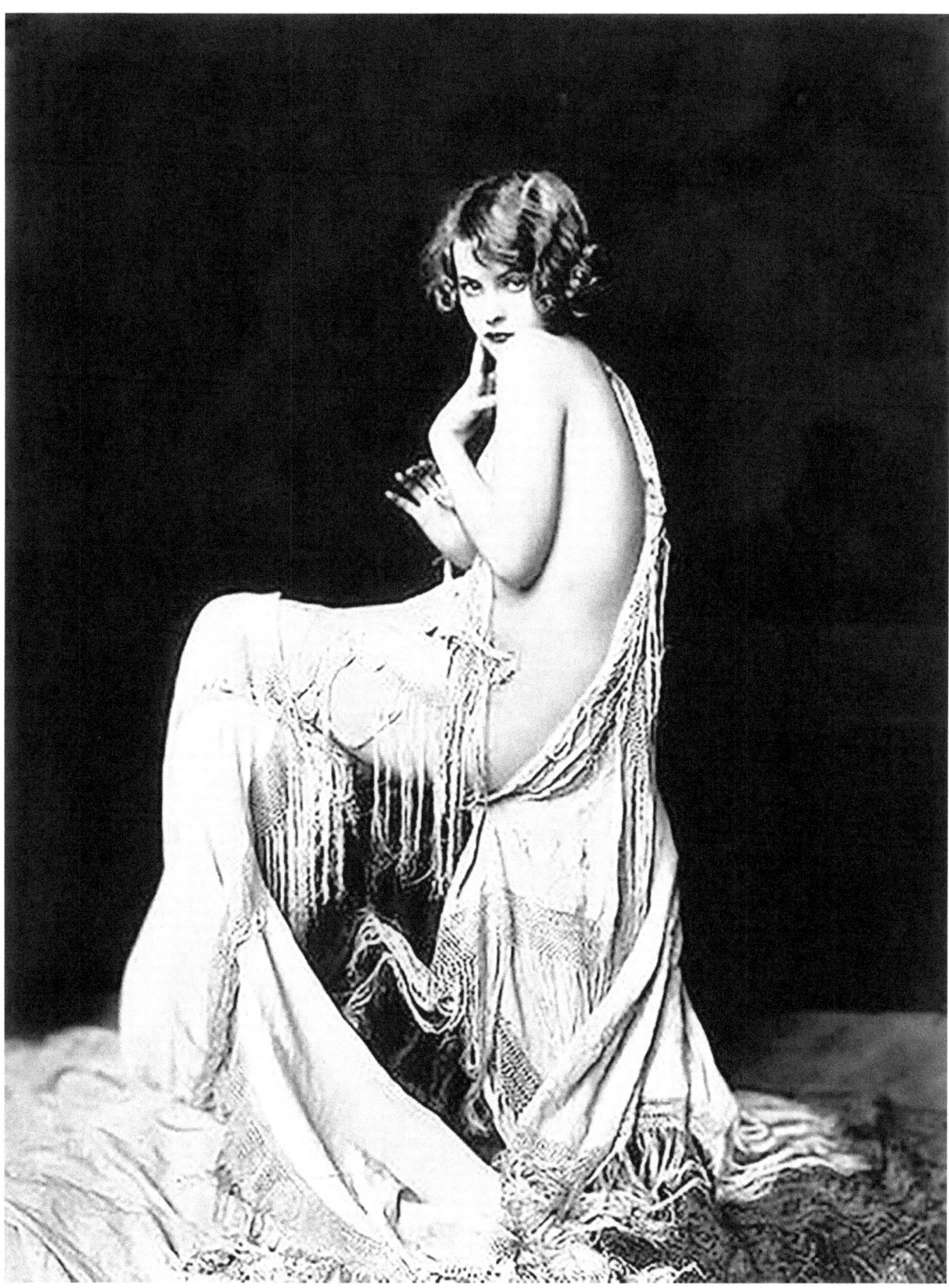

Ziegfeld girl with draped costume.

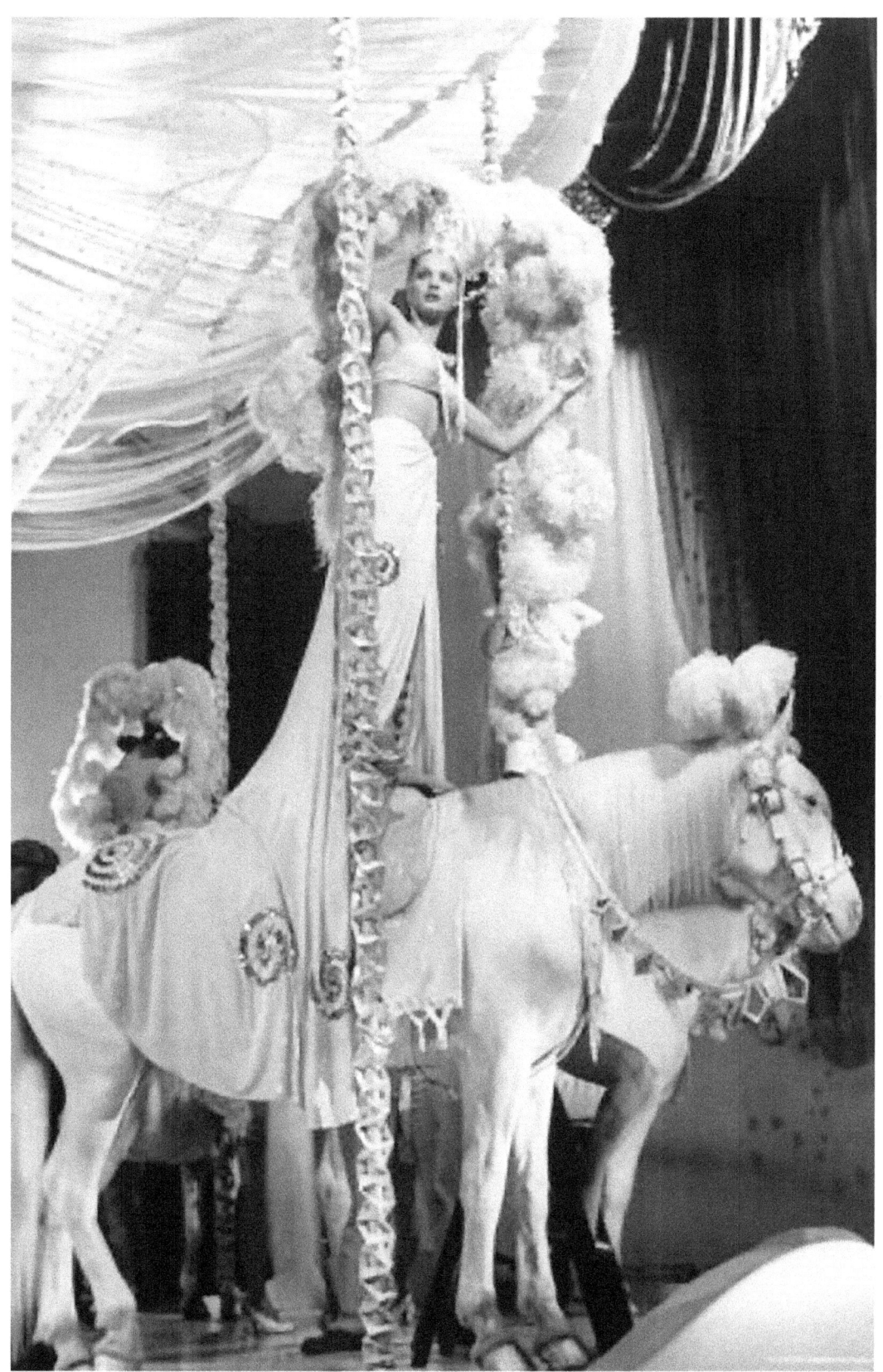

Ziegfeld girl (possibly Muriel Finlay) in very elaborate stage setting.

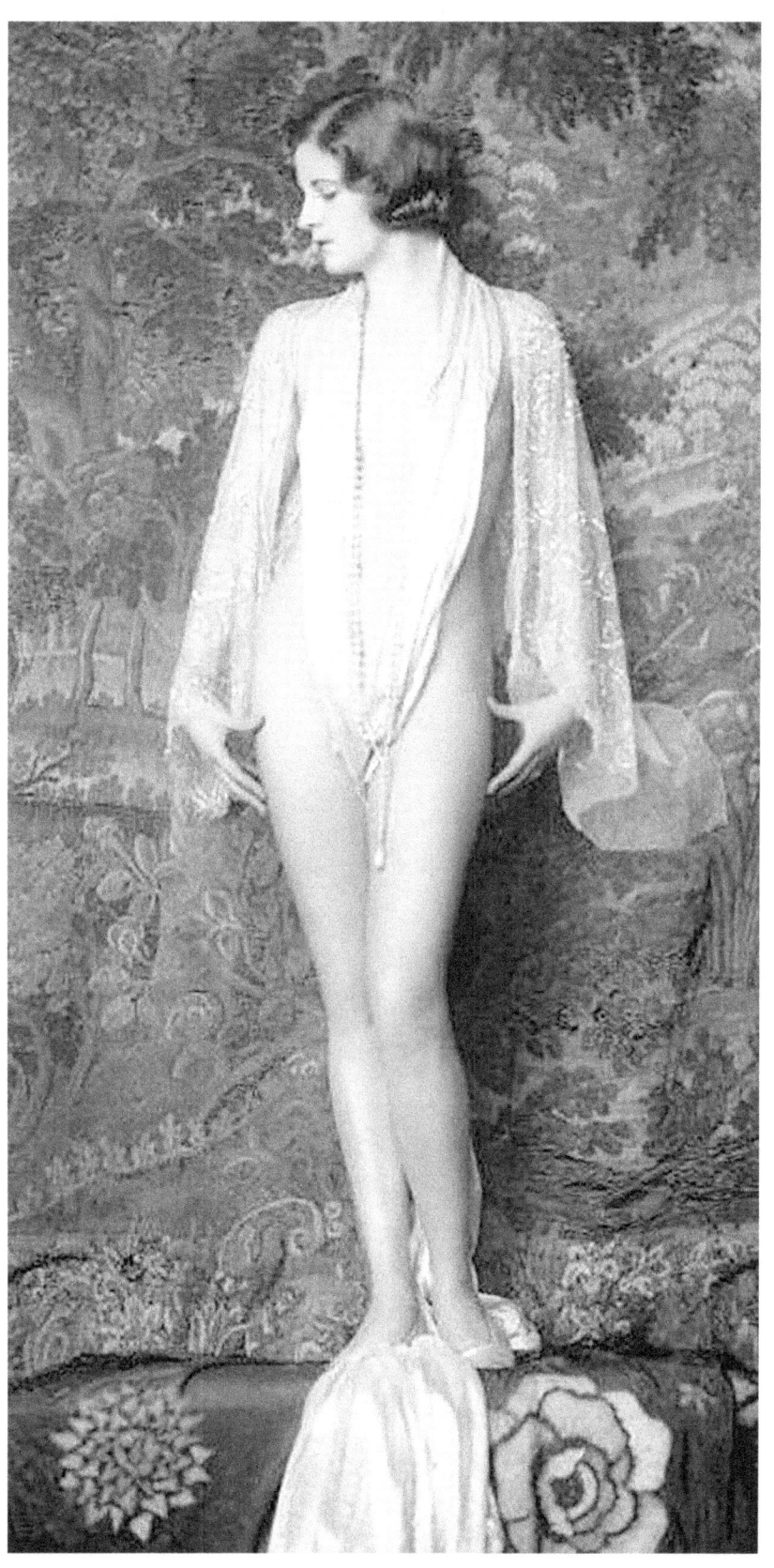

Olive Brady

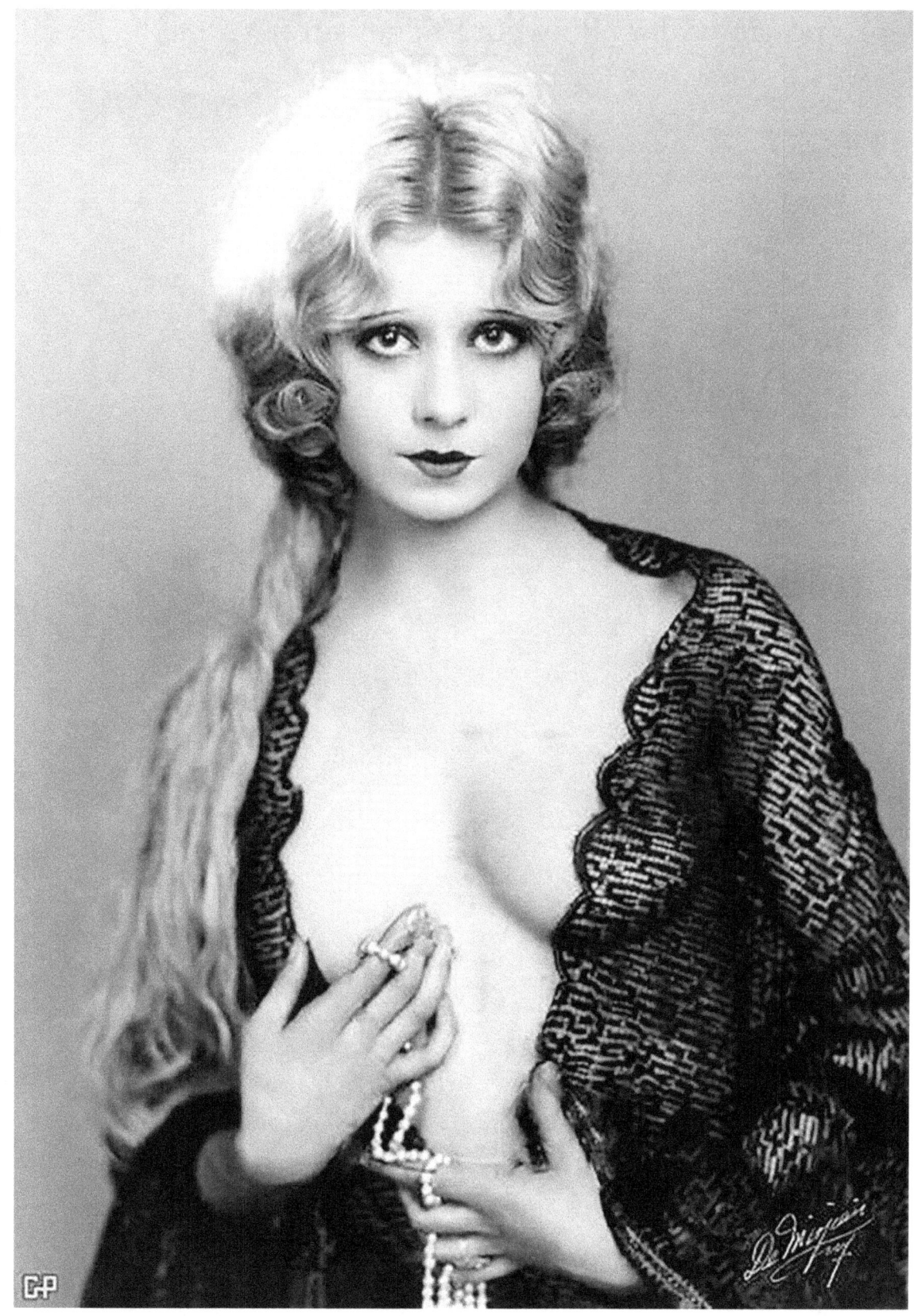

Ziegfeld girl (possibly Clara Bow but I'm not sure).

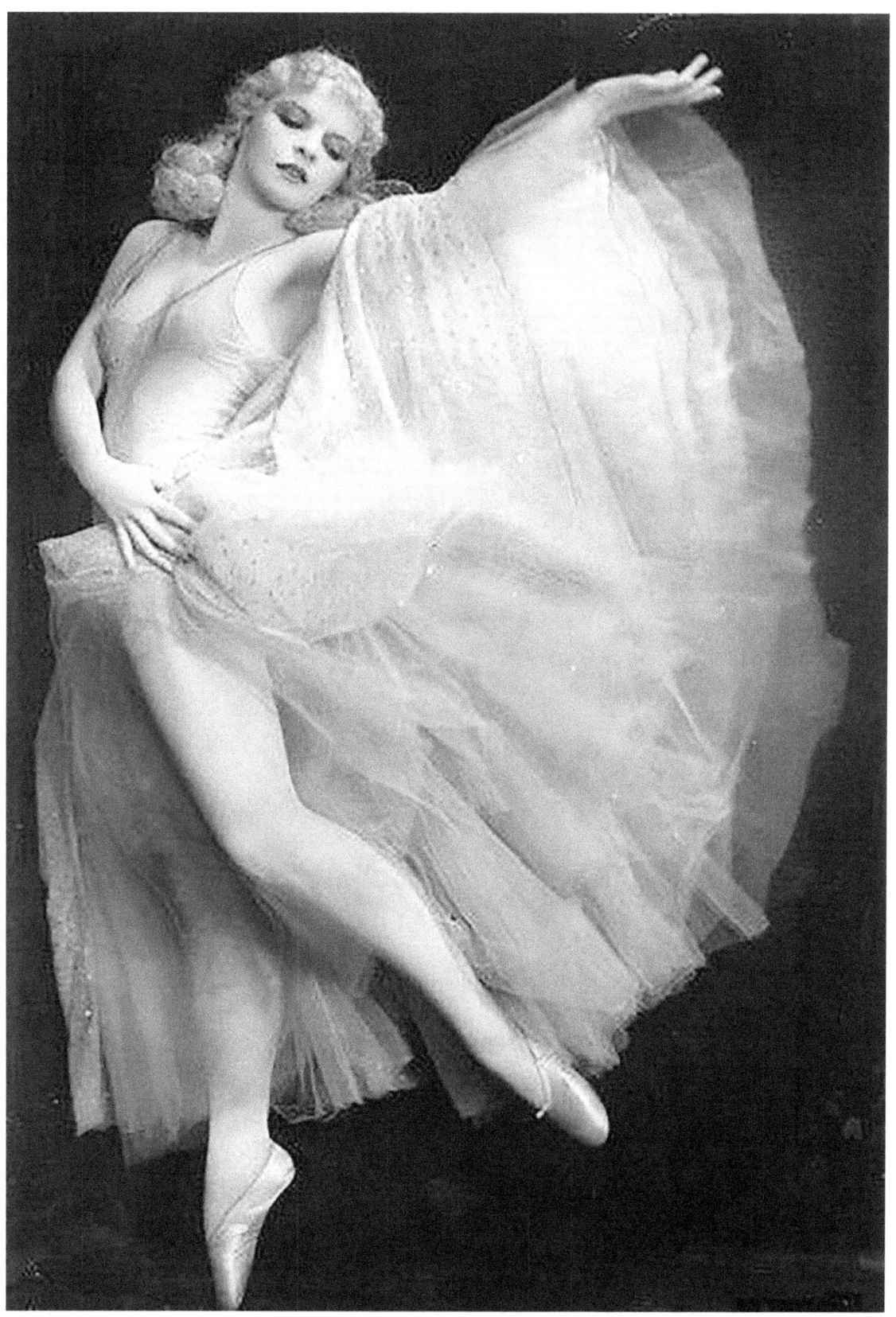

Ziegfeld girl

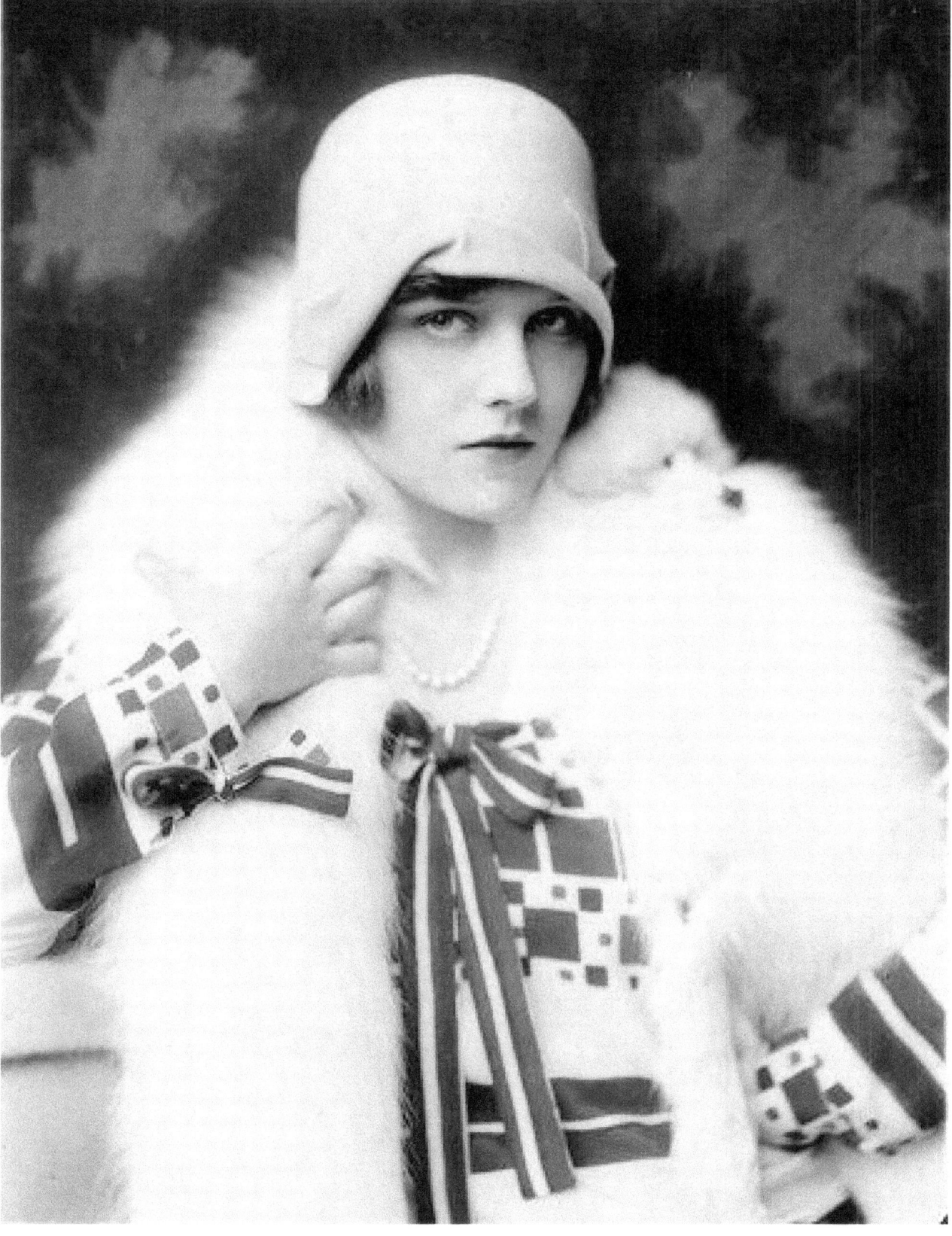

Naomi Johnson- Naomi Johnson ~ Performed in the Ziegfeld Follies of 1922, 1923 (Summer Edition), and 1925, Ziegfeld's musical "Rio Rita" (1927 – 1928), and in Ziegfeld's opera "The Three Musketeers" of 1928. Photo: Alfred Cheney Johnston.

www.ingramcontent.com/pod-product-compliance
Lightning Source LLC
Chambersburg PA
CBHW080614190526
45169CB00007B/3014